KETOGENIC BREAD COOKBOOK

KETOGENIC

BREAD

COOKBOOK

Complete Guide to Easy Low Carb Baking for Keto Dieters

Amber Gryffon

Contents

The ketogenic diet has been the catalyst for a whole new way of living in my house. Prior to my discovery of the ketosis effect, I lived my life much the same way as many people around me did. I ate what I thought was a healthy variety of food, not realizing that so many of the ingredients were causing me much more harm than good. For example, I never took into account that fruit shouldn't be eaten in limitless quantities just because it has the reputation of being healthy. Everything I ate was supposedly 'healthy', but in return I just kept getting bigger and feeling worse.

Switching over to the ketogenic diet helped me find a whole new appreciation for good food, and especially for food that my body loved and found easy to digest. There was one tiny problem though, **I missed bread**! In my haste to start the keto diet as soon as possible, I hadn't taken into account that generic bread consists almost entirely of carbohydrates.

Even with all of the great benefits of a keto diet, the absence of bread really hit me, and there were many times when I felt like giving up just because I couldn't have any bread with my food. I decided to do some serious online research to see if there was any way that I could overcome the absence of bread. But I found something even better, keto bread!

After reading just a few articles on the subject of the keto diet, it was already evident to me that **so many people were giving it up precisely because of an absence of bread** and how much they missed it. They would do everything else right, but as soon as the need for a slice of bread became too much to handle, they would ruin all of their hard work and end up falling right out of ketosis. What a shame it would be to let all of that hard work go to waste just because of a bread craving. Luckily, with so many ingredients available to us in the world, I soon realized that there was a way around the problem, and that bread could be made with ingredients that either had very little or no carbs in them whatsoever!

I worked hard to develop recipes that would contain less than 7g of net carbs per serving so that I could eat bread while staying in ketosis. As soon as I realized that there was a world of creativity behind this seemingly simple staple food, I knew I have to share my discovery with other keto dieters so that the world could share the joy of low-carb bread with me. What I got in return for my creativity was much more than just delicious recipes.

No additives ever found their way into my bread recipes. Commercial bread products tend to have not just high levels of carbs but also many artificial additives in them. Anything from color and flavoring additives to preservatives that make food last longer on the shelf. When I started making my own bread I also freed my body from all of these negative ingredients that were ruining my vitality and causing an imbalance in my digestion system and hormone levels.

I enjoyed bread with my meals without any feelings of guilt. Because the carb count of my bread recipes is so low, I was able to add bread back into my diet without experience any impact on my weight. It's fascinating how when you are restricted from something you suddenly want it more than ever. I was obsessed with the lack of bread in my life, and it nearly led me to disastrous situations of giving up keto entirely. But suddenly, after being able to prepare and eat my own low-carb ketogenic bread, the crazy cravings were gone. I can now enjoy a warm fresh baked bun, sliced loaf, or other type of bread, and also be proud of my new baking talent.

My ketosis remained intact. It's particularly true in the early beginnings of the keto diet that triggering and then staying in ketosis can be quite a challenge if you are completely new to it. Even the slightest mistake in food intake can force a stop to ketosis, preventing your body from burning fat, and instead going back to solely burning glucose. These changes are a negative influence on the psychology of what you are trying to achieve, because what is perceived as failure is often followed by defeat, which means that people are likely to give up after even the smallest of mistakes. However, when you have something as delicious as your own keto bread available in your diet, the need for commercial hamburgers, sandwiches, or bagels disappears, and you don't even notice that there may be something missing from the way you used to eat your food.

I became a lot more creative in the kitchen. Because I was able to create my own bread recipes, I suddenly felt a whole new surge of creativity in the kitchen. When you make something that is entirely your own, you have a much greater appreciation for the product, and you are also more likely to eat it at a slower pace, so that you can enjoy every moment of what you created. I developed recipes that were both sweet and savory, as well as recipes that I could easily adapt to the diets of my friends, which means that I was able to bring bread with me to family gatherings and dinners so that we could all enjoy it. I never felt left out of the dinner group because I was always able to contribute to the feast with my very own recipes.

Making my own bread helped to cement the ketogenic diet as a lifestyle. Bread lovers will understand when I tell them that not having to run away from bread makes any eating plan look normal. So as soon as I started making my own bread, I no longer felt like I was on any kind of diet. It was simply a way of life that was now healthier, and far more creative than it had ever been. So if you're a bread lover, stick around to see how these delicious bread recipes will make the most of your time on ketosis!

I hope you enjoy these recipes and that they help you to make the ketogenic diet a permanent lifestyle that is more enjoyable than ever before. Making my own low-carb bread has changed my life, and I humbly offer you this collection of recipes with the hope that it will change yours too.

Yours in good health,
Amber Gryffon

BREAD
gone keto

Scientifically speaking, the ketogenic diet, or keto diet, is one of the most researched diets in the world. Its procedure, application, and benefits are among the best established in the dietary world, and for good reason. In order to understand how this diet affects your body and why so many people swear by it, we must first answer a few questions regarding your own anatomy. Once you understand these points, it will become very clear why the keto diet has a worldwide following. Research is still conducted every year to find further benefits of ketosis on the human body, and the results are proving to be quite astounding.

WHAT EXACTLY IS THE KETOGENIC DIET?

Because we are now so frequently surrounded by and ingesting toxins in our body, eating a restricted diet which is free from these negative elements is like a breath of fresh air for your system. In terms of nutritive proportions in your daily food intake, the ketogenic diet is a high-fat, low-carbohydrate diet, with monitored protein intake (depending on age, height, and weight). Usually, an average person's diet has high levels of carbs with pretty much each meal, which means that their body burns those carbs as the primary energy source. It converts them into glucose (a type of sugar specifically used for energy), and uses it as the primary energy source. But once the carbs are quite drastically reduced in numbers, something new happens.

When the number of carbohydrates in the body is low, your system recognizes the deficiency and alerts the liver to convert fat into **ketone bodies** and fatty acids, and now uses those as the primary source of energy instead of the carbs. For the sake of clarity, we should explain what ketone bodies actually are. In the process of the metabolism of fats, three related compounds are released. Two of those compounds (acetoacetic acid and beta-Hydroxybutyric acid) are used as a source of energy, replacing glucose, while the third compound (Acetone) is simply excreted. Once the fatty acids and ketone bodies replace glucose, the body is able to continue all functions undisturbed with this new source of energy. This tipping point in a way of producing energy, is called **ketosis**.

THE KETO DIET ORIGINATED AS A SEMI-CURE FOR EPILEPSY

Unlike most diets, the keto diet's initial purpose was not weight loss, but instead a way to reduce the frequency of epileptic attacks in children, and even some adults. It was first developed in the early 1920s, when scientists discovered that an inadequate breakdown of glucose was one of the main causes of epileptic attacks. After discovering the incredible benefit of this diet on the epilepsy of his son, producer Jon Abrahams started the Charlie Foundation in the early 1990s to spread the word. The foundation was able to collect so much funding that it sponsored the creation of an entire research center in 1996, which exclusively dealt with finding a cure for epileptic seizures. Although medicine has certainly advanced since then, it is inspiring to know that this diet has truly had a effect on people's lives, allowing parents to suffer less anxiety about their child's struggles with epilepsy. The keto diet provided these families with a healthy, affordable alternative to pharmaceutical drugs, allowing their children an easier period of growth and development. Expanding your knowledge in the field of diets, as we have just done, allows you to have a new perspective on the word 'diet'. Although we have developed a world with endless food options to satisfy every imaginable craving, we easily forget that our bodies are often more likely to benefit from fewer food options than from an endless stream of it.

WHAT IS KETOSIS AND HOW TO ACHIEVE IT

We rarely give our bodies the credit they deserve when it comes to adapting to new situations and meal plans. Most people look to others to find a 'right' way to eat. But each body is different, and when you decide to change an aspect of your diet, your body will be right behind you to follow your progress all the way through.

In a regular scenario, the body would use the carbohydrates in your food to produce glucose and insulin. **Glucose** is used as the main energy source, while **insulin** acts as its guide, taking it around the body through the bloodstream. Unless you have very high levels of physical activity on a daily basis, your body will not use up all of the carbs that you've eaten, which means that it will never reach the stage where it will have any need for your fat stores as extra sources of energy. Now, here's what happens when you take away most of the carbs in your regular diet.

Step by Step Ketosis

1. Your body is surprised by the sudden low carb levels, but will still, curiously, continue to use glucose as its main source of energy.
2. Extend the low-carb diet to day 2, and now your body realizes that it is rapidly running out of an energy source. Will it panic? No, it will simply adjust, as it always does.
3. Your metabolism turns to your liver, and requests the start of the process of burning fat for fuel.
4. The liver is ready to act, and immediately starts producing ketone bodies by breaking down fat molecules.
5. This process, **ketosis,** is now the primary way for your body to turn the food you eat into energy.
6. Ketosis will continue until the liver senses an increased intake of carbohydrates, after which it will terminate ketosis, and go back to the use of glucose and insulin.

For those who are looking to lose weight, or simply burn extra fat, this is the process that accomplishes such a goal. People will often mistake this way of eating as 'starvation', but it is anything but. Your body is not starved for nutrients, energy, or vitamins and minerals. It is simply turning to a new chemical process of functioning.

WHAT ARE NET CARBS AND WHY YOU NEED TO COUNT THEM

By now we have established that the key to the ketogenic diet is low carb intake, which means that carbs need to be monitored and counted. But there are two ways to count carbs: Total Carbs and Net Carbs.

Total Carbs, as their name suggests, account for every single carbohydrate that you have eaten throughout the day. When people first develop an interest into the keto diet, they automatically feel as if all carbs must be counted throughout the day. This is an understandable assumption, but it isn't the right one, because such a notion completely disregards the existence and purpose of fibers.

Net Carbs are the total number of carbs that are consumed in a meal, minus the fibers. The reason why you should not count fibers in the keto diet is because fiber doesn't spike sugar levels, which also means that it doesn't affect ketosis. Fiber certainly has many beneficial points when it comes to your digestive system, but human beings simply do not digest it the way they do other nutrients, so it passes through the body without causing any side effects on ketosis.

This distinction between the two types of carb counting should be seen as a positive thing for people who love eating carbs, especially bread. As one of the highest carriers of carbs per serving, typical bread is both very difficult to remove from a diet, and yet also deliciously compliments every meal. When people transition over to a keto diet they often experience cravings for bread. But fear not, as this cookbook will teach you everything you need to know about **ketogenic bread**. All the delicious flavors of bread, but with less than 7g of net carbs!

TIPS FOR MAKING THE PERFECT KETOGENIC BREAD

Cooking is a science, quite literally. Remove even a single crucial ingredient and you will be left with a meal that looks nothing like the one you were promised in the picture. Likewise, add the wrong ingredient, and the whole thing could fall flat. When it comes to keto bread, delicious and beautiful as it is, it is created with ingredients that you likely haven't worked with before on a regular basis. It may take you a few tries before you get it right, but that's why this book is here to help you!

Helping Your Ketogenic Bread Rise

Bread is a recipe that needs to be made with love, care, and precision. It is made up of a number of different steps, all of which need to be done to perfection if the bread is to look, feel, and taste delicious. Because wheat is not part of the ketogenic diet, making bread without wheat seems like an instant problem. When combined with yeast, the two ingredients in combination are what makes the bread rise, which allows air to go inside the dough and make it light and fluffy. Bread without wheat, if not done properly, will end up being flat and unappealing visually. If you are to create delicious hamburgers and sandwiches with keto bread, you need to master the art of making bread rise without the aid of wheat. But don't worry, there are plenty of things that will help you do this, it just takes a little bit of practice.

Luckily, there are a few tricks you can use to create a rising effect even without the traditional ingredients.

1. **Acid-base reactions**: The 'rise' that we are looking for is basically just a need to generate carbon dioxide (CO_2). You can temper your dry and wet ingredients with additional elements so that when they mix together they create the rising effect. In your dry ingredients, add either baking soda or sodium bicarbonate. In your wet ingredients, add citric acid, lemon juice, or vinegar. Always remember to carefully follow the recipe in terms of amounts. When you then combine your wet ingredients and dry ingredients, you will generate carbon dioxide, which will give your keto dough a beautiful rising effect.
2. **Cream of tartar in egg whites**: Outside of the cooking world, cream of tartar is known as Potassium bitartrate and is a byproduct of wine making. Adding cream of tartar to egg whites makes them stable, which means that they won't lose their fluffy texture as soon as you stop whipping them. Combining the egg whites with the flour of your choice will then give the dough a wonderful, ready-to-bake texture that will look exactly like bread in the end.

Create the Perfect Mix for Your Bread

How you treat the mixture, and even the pan, of your bread is crucial to how it will turn out. Although each recipe is different, and I certainly advise you to follow it to the highest levels of precision, the truth is that ketogenic bread needs a delicate touch in order to be the best bread that it can be. Here are some great general tips on making the perfect mixture for your ketogenic bread:

1. The first step to delicious bread is **making sure that your oven is preheated and that you've lined your pan with some oil and parchment paper**. The reason why bread works best when inserted into a super hot oven as opposed to a cold one is because the rising elements react with the heat immediately. If you were to put the dough into a cold oven, by the time the heat rises enough to begin the activation process for $CO2$, the dough has fallen flat and is no longer able to have the same reaction.
2. **Mix the egg whites and the egg yolks separately**. Egg whites are a lot fluffier when whipped on their own, and we've already established that you need all the air available to make the keto bread as fluffy as possible.
3. **Mix all of the dry ingredients into a separate bowl first**. Dry ingredients can be of different textures and grain sizes, so if you mix them all together first you reduce the chance of the dough mixture being grainy. You will notice that some recipes may call for the dry ingredients to be blended together first in a sort of flour texture. This is because it will give them an extra boost and make the whole thing a lot smoother.
4. Once the bread is out of the oven, grab the parchment paper and carefully **place the bread onto a cooling rack**. This will ensure that the bread doesn't become moist, and instead slowly hardens into a beautiful bread shape that will later be easy to slice.
5. **Make sure to follow every single step of the recipe**. Weigh everything correctly, follow the correct order of ingredient mixture, and of course make sure to correctly set the temperature and the time of the bake. Even the smallest of mistakes can make the whole thing fall to peaces.

How to Avoid Common Mistakes

1. When it comes to choosing the correct pan to bake your keto bread in, **do not use a silicon pan**. It may be a favorite for people who use wheat and yeast in their recipes, but for keto bread is it a horrible dish of choice because the bread will not rise properly. Instead, use a proper firm pan so that the bread is exposed to maximum heat.

2. **Do not over mix your dough!** You are very likely to end up with a hollow crust if you do so, because the dough will instantly deflate. Only mix the ingredients until they form an even texture, and then make sure to let the dough rest for at least 30 minutes before placing it in the oven.

3. If you don't use any nuts in your recipe, you may experience the **baking paper sticking to the bread**. There are two ways to deal with this. The first option is to let the bread cool down completely, and to then remove the paper once the bread has completely cooled. If this doesn't work, you can place a wet towel over the paper to soften it a little before removing it.

Making keto bread isn't difficult, but it certainly requires practice, and perhaps most importantly, an understanding of a new set of staples and how they work. In a traditional kitchen, most of the staples that are used have very high levels of carbohydrates in them, which means that things that you are used to from past baking experiences will now be replaced by new products that behave differently in the kitchen. Their measurements, temperatures, and pairings with other ingredients is very different from your regular flour and sugar mix. But there is no need to worry, because we have compiled a full list of ingredients that you will frequently be using, so that you can instantly become familiar with them. After a few test runs you will easily become an expert in the field of keto bread baking!

Flours and Additives

The following is a list of some of the most frequent main ingredients that you will find in keto bread recipes. They aren't as difficult to use as they may seem at first glance, so becoming familiar with these ingredients will allow you to be incredibly creative in the kitchen. Once you understand the basics of how these ingredients work and how they can be mixed together to create a whole new array of flavors, it will be very easy for you to experiment with your own recipes. But before you go wild in the kitchen, let's first start with the basics.

Egg White Protein

Protein is already an important part of the keto diet (moderate to each individual), so including it in your recipe will become an extra source of nutrients that your body needs anyway. Egg white protein is easy to find, inexpensive, and adds a smooth, compact texture to bread recipes. Protein allows the dough to form into its final shape, and to keep that shape during the cooking process. The great thing about this ingredient is that you will never need too much of it. Protein is good for you but it is not something that you should eat in crazy amounts, because once you cross the amount of protein that your body needs, the rest of it will be wasted. Whipping up egg whites on their own is a great, fluffy addition to your dough recipe, but egg white protein in powdered form gives it that extra boost that egg whites on their own simply cannot match.

Xanthan Gum

If this ingredient sounds scientific, it's because it really is quite the scientific mix, usually used in molecular gastronomy. Its most common usage in powder form is as a thickener and a stabilizer. This ingredient is gluten free and also net carb free, which makes it the perfect addition to any bread recipe. You only need small amounts of this fascinating ingredient because it will go a long way in helping you achieve the perfect bread recipe. It lasts for a very long time and is usually found in any large supermarket or health food store.

Psyllium Husk

This is another seemingly exotic ingredient that few people cook with but that has incredible overall benefits for the human body. Essentially, psyllium husk is a type of fiber, which is extracted from the Plantago ovata seeds; a plant which is native to Western and Southern Asia. The magic of this particular ingredient is that it can make any keto flour taste like regular wheat flour. Apart from changing the flavor of the dough to a familiar wheat grain flavor, it also gives it a somewhat grainy texture which is also reminiscent of the regular flour bread. Because it is high in fiber, you only need small amounts to make a real difference to your recipe, and also, it is very beneficial for your digestive system. Your digestive system doesn't really need to absorb fiber or to break it down, but what it does use it for is easier digestion and the cleaning of your intestines. It's a shame that most people discover this wonderful ingredient only once they have discovered the keto diet, so if you know someone who is looking for healthy digestion support, recommend them the psyllium husk.

Coconut Flour

There is a slight aversion when people hear that coconut flour is used for savory bread, because they feel that it will taste of coconut no matter what the recipe ingredients are. However, coconut flour on its own doesn't have as strong of a coconut flavor as people are used to finding in chocolate bars and cakes. It is incredibly absorptive and can also be used as a thickening agent. Add any other ingredient with coconut flour and you will soon realize that this amazing product is a mastermind of combining textures and flavors, and it will become difficult to imagine your keto baking life without it. As a bonus, it is also rich in protein, fiber, and healthy fats. The perfect addition to keto bread.

Almond Flour

One of the most elegant flour sources, almond flour is very low in carbohydrates and very high in healthy fats. Its rich taste will make any bread recipe better, and because it's made from almond seeds, every bread recipe made from this product will have an incredibly smooth texture. Almond flour is not famous for rising on its own, so you will need the help of egg whites and other keto bread ingredients to add airiness to your recipe. However, with just a little bit of practice, you will be on your way to making extraordinary bread recipes which feature almond flour.

Sesame Flour

Sesame flour has its own personality when it comes to bread making because it has a unique flavor which, quite literally, sticks to the back of your tongue. Its somewhat bitter flavor makes it a great ingredient for savory bread recipes, especially because it requires few additional ingredients in order to create a complete bread. It is also not a temperamental ingredient, so you will not have to care as much for its ability to rise and form a texture. You need simply add the appropriate amount to any bread recipe and give it a gentle stir until all of the ingredients are properly combined.

Flaxseed Meal

Flaxseed meal is a popular alternative to regular flour because it is low in carbohydrates and high in fiber. It has a strong flavor, which is why it is so frequently used in savory recipes. It doesn't like to rise much, so you will need the help of other ingredients to really make it shine.

Coconut Oil

Every bread recipe needs a stable oil ingredient to combine all of the other ingredients together, and also to withstand the high oven temperatures without releasing any toxins that the human body doesn't like to deal with. Coconut oil is a great substitute for regular oil and has a number of health benefits, such as burning fat, controlling your appetite, and lowering cholesterol. It has a very high heat point, so any bread recipe made with this ingredient will come out looking great and tasting delicious. Like coconut flour, many people connect this ingredient with sweet recipes only, but coconut oil is incredibly adaptive to other ingredients, and can easily be turned into a savory dish.

Organic Ghee

Ghee is a type of clarified butter, in a process which requires water to be evaporated and the fatty acids to be separated from the milk solids. It is different from regular clarified butter because it is simmered before reaching its completed stage, which means that it has a nutty flavor. This is wonderful as an additional ingredient to any bread recipe because it gives it a depth of flavor that would otherwise be difficult to extract from any other ingredient. Although it originated in Southeast Asia where it is a regular staple in many kitchens, ghee has slowly made its way into the Western world as well, enriching traditional Western recipes with its very unique taste.

Coconut Mana

This will easily become your new favorite butter! Coconut mana is a natural, unsweetened product which is made directly from the meat of the coconut. Although some people advise that you could technically make this on your own in a food processor from the flesh of an actual coconut, it is a better idea to purchase a ready-made one from your health store because it takes a lot of machine power to make sure that the coconut mana has a completely smooth texture. This ensures that your dough will not have any unwanted grainy elements, which is something that you probably wouldn't be able to achieve in a regular food processor. It is very high in fat and one of the most keto-friendly ingredients currently available.

LOAVES

Contents

Best Keto Bread

Serves: 20 / Preparation time: 10 minutes / Cooking time: 30 minutes

The egg whites and egg yolks are separated to produce a nice and fluffy loaf. The soft peaks produced when beating the egg whites add volume to the bread.

6 large eggs (separated)

1 ½ cups almond flour

4 tablespoons butter (melted)

3 teaspoons baking powder

¼ teaspoon cream of tartar

1 pinch salt

- Preheat oven to 375F.
- Separate egg whites from the egg yolks. Beat egg whites and cream of tartar.
- Mix egg yolks, 1/3 beaten egg whites, almond flour, butter, baking powder and salt in a food processor.
- Add remaining 2/3 egg whites on the food processor. Gently process and do not overmix.
- Pour mixture in a loaf pan. Bake for 30 minutes.

PER SERVING: Calories: 90; Fat: 8g; Protein: 4g; Carbs: 2g; Fiber: 1g Net Carbs: 1g; Fat 78% / Protein 18% / Carbs 4%

Keto Bread with Xanthan Gum

The xanthan gum binds the ingredients well. It prevents the bread from crumbling easily.

7 eggs

2 cups almond flour

½ cup butter (melted)

2 tablespoons coconut oil

1 teaspoon baking powder

½ teaspoon xanthan gum

½ teaspoon salt

- Preheat oven to 355F.
- Beat eggs in a bowl for 2 minutes.
- Add butter and oil, continue beating.
- Add almond flour, baking powder, xanthan gum and salt.
- Pour mixture in a lined loaf pan.
- Bake for 45 minutes.
- Let it cool for a few minutes then slice.

PER SERVING: Calories: 278; Fat: 28g; Protein: 9g; Carbs: 5g; Fiber: 3g
Net Carbs: 2g; Fat 88% / Protein 9% / Carbs 3%

Paleo Keto Cornbread

Mixing the eggs using a blender gives it volume. The bread can be grilled and covered with butter.

4 eggs

1 cup water

½ cup coconut flour

¼ cup coconut oil (melted)

2 tablespoons apple cider vinegar

½ teaspoon baking soda

½ teaspoon garlic powder

¼ teaspoon sea salt (coarse)

- Crack open the eggs in the blender. Let sit for 20 minutes.
- Put water, coconut oil and apple cider vinegar in the blender. Blend for 30 seconds.
- Put coconut flour, baking soda, garlic powder and salt in the blender. Blend for 1 minute.
- Coat baking pan with coconut oil.
- Pour mixture in the pan. Bake for 45 minutes at 350F.

**PER SERVING: Calories: 98; Fat: 7g; Protein: 3g; Carbs: 4g; Fiber: 3g
Net Carbs: 1g; Fat 81% / Protein 15% / Carbs 4%**

Cinnamon Bread

For dairy-free recipe, coconut milk can be used as a substitute for Greek yogurt and coconut oil plus salt can be used as substitute for salted butter.

3 eggs (pastured)

½ cup coconut flour

1/3 cup Greek yogurt

3 tablespoons butter (salted)

2 tablespoons water

1 teaspoon cinnamon

1 teaspoon vinegar

½ teaspoon baking powder

½ teaspoon baking soda

1/8 teaspoon stevia

- Preheat oven to 350F. Prepare loaf pan by lining it with parchment paper.
- Put coconut flour, cinnamon, baking powder, baking soda and stevia in the blender. Mix thoroughly.
- Put yogurt, butter, water and vinegar in the blender. Mix well.
- Let it sit for 3 minutes. Blend again.
- Pour mixture in the pan. Bake for 30 minutes.
- Cool then store in the fridge.

PER SERVING: Calories: 90; Fat: 7g; Protein: 3g; Carbs: 5g; Fiber: 3g
Net Carbs: 2g; Fat 74% / Protein 17% / Carbs 9%

Microwave Paleo Bread

Serves: 4 / Preparation time: 3 minutes / Cooking time: 2 minutes

This is a basic recipe that can be spiced up with some fruit or seasoning. This can be served with a hot bowl of chili, paleo jam or soup.

1 egg (whisked)

1/3 cup almond flour

2 ½ tablespoons ghee (melted)

½ teaspoon baking powder

1/8 teaspoon salt

- Coat mug with ghee.
- Put all ingredients in a bowl. Mix thoroughly using a fork.
- Put mixture in a mug.
- Microwave on high for 90 seconds.
- Let it cool for a few minutes.
- Remove from mug carefully. Slice.

**PER SERVING: Calories: 132; Fat: 13g; Protein: 3g; Carbs: 2g; Fiber: 1g
Net Carbs: 1g; Fat 88% / Protein 9% / Carbs 3%**

Paleo Bread

Either olive oil or coconut oil can be used in this recipe. Bread with olive oil goes well with salty foods while bread with coconut oil goes well with sweet foods.

3 eggs

3 cups almond flour

½ cup + 2 tablespoons olive oil

¼ cup almond milk

2 teaspoons baking powder

1 teaspoon baking soda

¼ teaspoon salt

- Preheat oven to 300F.
- Coat loaf pan with olive oil.
- Put all ingredients in a bowl. Mix thoroughly.
- Pour mixture in the pan and spread evenly.
- Bake for 1 hour.
- Let it cool for a few minutes then slice.

PER SERVING: Calories: 580; Fat: 59g; Protein: 10g; Carbs: 9g; Fiber: 4g Net Carbs: 5g; Fat 90% / Protein 7% / Carbs 3%

Keto Bread Loaves

Keto bread loaves can be served with butter, ghee or cream cheese. It can also be used in sandwiches.

6 large eggs

1 cup coconut flour (sifted)

½ cup flaxseed meal

½ cup water

1 tablespoon apple cider vinegar

1 teaspoon baking powder

1 teaspoon salt

½ teaspoon baking soda

- Preheat oven to 350F. Coat baking pan with oil.
- Mix coconut flour, flaxseed meal, baking powder, salt and baking soda in a bowl.
- Add egg, water and vinegar. Mix thoroughly.
- Put mixture in a coated pan. Bake for 40 minutes.
- Let it cool for a few minutes then slice.

**PER SERVING: Calories: 134; Fat: 8g; Protein: 8g; Carbs: 11g; Fiber: 8g
Net Carbs: 3g; Fat 64% / Protein 27% / Carbs 9%**

Keto Almond Bread

Almond flour is beneficial to your health. It helps control blood sugar and cholesterol levels.

2 eggs (whisked)

1 cup almond flour

3 tablespoons olive oil

1 ½ teaspoons baking powder

1 teaspoon fine salt

1 teaspoon mustard powder

- Preheat oven to 350F.
- Put eggs, almond flour, olive oil, baking powder, salt and mustard powder. Mix thoroughly.
- Pour mixture into a baking pan.
- Bake for 30 minutes.
- Let it cool then cut into 4 thick slices.

PER SERVING: Calories: 257; Fat: 24g; Protein: 8g; Carbs: 5g; Fiber: 3g
Net Carbs: 2g; Fat 84% / Protein 12% / Carbs 3%

Pumpkin and Orange Cheese Bread

Serves: 12 / Preparation time: 15 minutes / Cooking time: 1 hour

The recipe requires moisture to prevent the bread from drying. Water bath is done by placing a baking dish with water in the oven while cooking.

For the bread:

4 large eggs

2 cups almond flour

¾ cup pumpkin (puree)

½ cup Erythritol

¼ cup butter (melted)

1 tablespoon fresh orange zest

2 teaspoons pumpkin pie spice mix

½ teaspoon cream of tartar

¼ teaspoon baking soda

15 drops liquid Stevia extract

For the cheese topping:

1 large egg

3 cups cream cheese

½ cup pumpkin puree

¼ cup Erythritol

1 tablespoon natural orange extract

½ teaspoon cinnamon

Juice form ½ average orange

10 drops liquid Stevia extract

Pinch of salt

- Preheat oven to 300F.
- Mix almond flour, pumpkin pie spice mix, cream of tartar and baking soda in a bowl.
- Beat eggs, Erythritol, butter and Stevia in a separate bowl.
- Combine the egg mixture with the dry mixture. Add pumpkin puree. Mix thoroughly. Add fresh orange zest.
- Mix topping ingredients: egg, cream cheese, Erythritol, orange juice and Stevia in a separate bowl. Add orange extract.
- Spoon the bread batter into a baking dish. Spread evenly using a ladle.
- Add a layer of half of the cheese mixture on top of the bread batter. Spread evenly.
- Mix the other half of the cheese mixture with pumpkin puree and cinnamon.
- Spoon the pumpkin cheese mixture on top of the batter. Spread evenly.
- Bake for 1 hour in an oven with water bath.
- Let it cool down. Remove from baking dish and serve.

PER SERVING: Calories: 300; Fat: 29g; Protein: 10g; Carbs: 9g; Fiber: 3g Net Carbs: 6g; Fat 81% / Protein 12% / Carbs 7%

Low Carb Soul Bread

Serves: 16 / Preparation time: 10 minutes / Cooking time: 45 minutes

Whey protein is used as a substitute for a low carb flour. Stevia drops is an optional ingredient that can be added as a flavor enhancer.

4 eggs

12 ounces cream cheese (softened)

1 2/3 cups whey protein (unflavored)

¼ cup butter

¼ cup heavy whipping cream

¼ cup olive oil

2 ½ teaspoons baking powder

1 teaspoon xanthan gum

½ teaspoon salt

1/3 teaspoon baking soda

¼ teaspoon cream of tartar

- Preheat oven to 325F. Coat bread pan with oil.
- Microwave cream cheese and butter for 1 minute.
- Mix well using a blender.
- Add eggs, heavy cream and olive well. Mix thoroughly.
- Mix all dry ingredients: whey protein, baking powder, xanthan hum, salt, baking soda and cream of tartar in a separate bowl.
- Add dry mixture to the cream cheese mixture. Mix thoroughly using a spatula.
- Pour batter into the bread pan. Bake for 45 minutes.

PER SERVING: Calories: 200; Fat: 15g; Protein: 10g; Carbs: 2g; Fiber: 1g
Net Carbs: 1g; Fat 75% / Protein 22% / Carbs 3%

Cream Cheese Bread

Peanut flour is like coconut flour which is highly absorbent. You need less flour when baking breads which results to fewer calories.

4 large egg yolks

5 ounces cream cheese

½ cup peanut flour

4 tablespoons butter (melted)

2 tablespoons brown sugar

1 teaspoon baking powder

1 teaspoon vanilla

salt

- Combine cream cheese and butter. Mix thoroughly using a hand mixer.
- Add egg yolks, sugar, baking powder, vanilla and salt to the mixture. Mix thoroughly.
- Add peanut flour. Mix until thick.
- Pour batter into a coatedloaf pan. Bake for 25 minutes at 350F.

**PER SERVING: Calories: 88; Fat: 8g; Protein: 3g; Carbs: 2g; Fiber: 0g
Net Carbs: 2g; Fat 80% / Protein 12% / Carbs 8%**

Keto Seeded Bread

Keto seeded bread can be made into a steak sandwich. The bread can be toasted and eaten as is.

7 eggs

2 cups almond flour

½ cup butter

¼ cup sunflower seeds

3 tablespoons sesame seeds

2 tablespoons chia seeds

2 tablespoons coconut oil

1 teaspoon baking powder

½ teaspoon salt

½ teaspoon xanthium gum

- Preheat oven to 350F.
- Beat eggs in a bowl for 2 minutes. Add xanthium gum. Continue beating.
- Add coconut oil and butter. Continue beating.
- Add almond flour, sunflower seeds, chia seeds, baking powder and salt.
- Mix until thick. Put mixture into a loaf pan. Place sesame seeds on top.
- Bake for 40 minutes.

**PER SERVING: Calories: 405; Fat: 37g; Protein: 14g; Carbs: 5g; Fiber: 1g
Net Carbs: 4g; Fat 82% / Protein 14% / Carbs 4%**

Keto Banana Bread

Banana extract is used as a substitute for banana since it is not allowed in a ketogenic diet. Banana extract tastes like banana without the carbs that banana carries.

7 eggs

2 cups almond flour

½ cup butter (melted)

¼ cup Erythritol

¼ cup sunflower seeds

2 tablespoons chia seeds

2 tablespoons olive oil

2 tablespoons sesame seeds for topping

1 teaspoon baking powder (aluminum free)

½ teaspoon salt

½ teaspoon xanthium gum

4 drops banana extract

- Preheat oven to 355F.
- Beat eggs in a bowl for 2 minutes. Add butter and olive oil. Continue beating.
- Add almond flour, Erythritol, sunflower seeds, chia seeds, baking powder, salt, xanthium gum and banana extract.
- Mix until thick. Put mixture into a loaf pan. Place sesame seeds on top.
- Bake for 45 minutes.

**PER SERVING: Calories: 400; Fat: 37g; Protein: 14g; Carbs: 6g; Fiber: 2g
Net Carbs: 4g; Fat 82% / Protein 14% / Carbs 4%**

Keto Coconut Bread

Serves: 16 / Preparation time: 10 minutes / Cooking time: 45 minutes

This is a nut free recipe that can be eaten by people allergic to nuts. To make this dairy free, substitute butter with olive oil.

7 large eggs

½ cup butter

½ cup coconut flour

1 teaspoon baking soda (aluminum free)

½ teaspoon salt

½ teaspoon xanthan gum

- Preheat oven to 355F.
- Beat eggs in a bowl for 2 minutes.
- Add butter, coconut flour, baking soda, salt and xanthan gum. Continue beating.
- Put mixture into a loaf pan.
- Bake for 45 minutes.

**PER SERVING: Calories: 193; Fat: 16g; Protein: 6g; Carbs: 3g; Fiber: 2g
Net Carbs: 1g; Fat 81% / Protein 15% / Carbs 4%**

Low Carb Rye Bread

Serves: 16 / Preparation time: 15 minutes / Cooking time: 1 hour

This bread is always a bit moist. Toast the bread to remove moisture.

<u>Dry ingredients:</u>

2 cups flaxseed (ground)

1 cup coconut flour

2 tablespoons caraway seeds

1 tablespoon + 1 teaspoon baking powder

1 tablespoon Erythritol

¼ cup chia seeds (ground)

1 teaspoon salt to taste

<u>Wet ingredients:</u>

8 eggs (separated)

1 cup water (warm)

½ cup grass-fed ghee (softened not melted)

1/3 cup apple cider vinegar

2 tablespoons sesame oil (toasted)

- Preheat oven to 350F.
- Add dry ingredients in a bowl. Mix thoroughly.
- Separate egg yolks from egg whites. Set aside the egg whites.
- Add softened ghee and toasted sesame oil to the egg yolks. Mix until smooth.
- Beat egg whites in a separate bowl until soft peaks are produced.
- Add dry mixture to the egg yolk mixture. Mix thoroughly.
- Add vinegar and mix.
- Add warm water and mix.
- Add egg whites and gently mix.
- Put batter into a large coated loaf pan. Smooth evenly using a spatula.
- Bake for 1 hour.
- Let it cool then slice.

PER SERVING: Calories: 256; Fat: 21g; Protein: 8g; Carbs: 9g; Fiber: 7g Net Carbs: 2g; Fat 82% / Protein 15% / Carbs 3%

Multipurpose Flax-free and Nut-free Bread

Serves: 14 / Preparation time: 15 minutes / Cooking time: 1 hour 10 minutes

You can top this bread with butter, cream cheese, sliced ham and cheese or home-made ham. Remaining slices can be placed in a freezer for up to 3 months.

Wet ingredients:

8 large egg whites

2 large eggs

2 cups water (boiling)

Dry ingredients:

1 ½ cups sesame seed flour

1 cup coconut flour

1/3 cup psyllium husk powder

1 tablespoon baking powder (gluten-free)

1 teaspoon salt

- Preheat oven to 350F. Coat loaf pan with ghee then line with parchment paper.
- Mix whole eggs and egg whites in a bowl using a fork. Set aside.
- Combine all dry ingredients in a bowl. Mix thoroughly.
- Add the egg mixture to the dry mixture. Mix until thick.
- Add boiling water. Mix well.
- Put dough into the lined loaf pan.
- Bake for 1 hour and 15 minutes.
- Let it cool then cut into 12 slices.

PER SERVING: Calories: 103; Fat: 4g; Protein: 10g; Carbs: 8g; Fiber: 6g Net Carbs: 2g; Fat 44% / Protein 45% / Carbs 11%

BREADSTICKS

Contents

Keto Italian Style Breadsticks

These breadsticks are already savory and can be just dipped in tomato sauce. This is best served warm but if you'll store it for later consumption, you can put them in the fridge and broil for a few minutes before serving.

For the breadstick base:

1 large egg

2 cups mozzarella cheese

¾ cup almond flour

3 tablespoons cream cheese

1 tablespoon psyllium husk powder

1 teaspoon baking powder

For the Italian style flavorings:

2 tablespoons Italian seasoning

1 teaspoon pepper

1 teaspoon salt

- Preheat oven to 400 F.
- Mix egg and cream cheese in bowl.
- Mix the dry ingredients: almond flour, psyllium husk powder and baking powder in a separate bowl.
- Microwave mozzarella cheese until sizzling.
- Mix egg, cream cheese and dry ingredients into the mozzarella cheese.
- Mold the dough together and press flat.
- Combine Italian style flavorings ingredients.
- Put the dough on foil. Cut using a pizza cutter.
- Season with the Italian style flavorings.
- Bake for 15 minutes. Serve while warm.

PER SERVING: Calories: 238; Fat: 19g; Protein: 13g; Carbs: 5g; Fiber: 3g Net Carbs: 2g; Fat 73% / Protein 23% / Carbs 4%

Keto Extra Cheesy Breadsticks

Serves: 6 / Preparation time: 10 minutes / Cooking time: 15 minutes

You can serve these breadsticks with some marinara. You can substitute the psyllium husk powder with flaxseed meal if not available.

For the breadstick base:

1 large egg

2 cups mozzarella cheese

¾ cup almond flour

3 tablespoons cream cheese

1 tablespoon psyllium husk powder

1 teaspoon baking powder

For the extra cheesy flavorings:

¼ cup parmesan cheese

3 ounces cheddar cheese

1 teaspoon garlic powder

1 teaspoon onion powder

- Preheat oven to 400 F.
- Mix egg and cream cheese in bowl.
- Mix the dry ingredients: almond flour, psyllium husk powder and baking powder in a separate bowl.
- Microwave mozzarella cheese until sizzling.
- Mix egg, cream cheese and dry ingredients into the mozzarella cheese.
- Mold the dough together and press flat.
- Combine extra cheesy flavorings ingredients.
- Put the dough on foil. Cut using a pizza cutter.
- Season with the extra cheesy flavorings.
- Bake for 15 minutes. Serve while warm.

PER SERVING: Calories: 314; Fat: 25g; Protein: 18g; Carbs: 6g; Fiber: 3g Net Carbs: 3g; Fat 73% / Protein 23% / Carbs 4%

Keto Sweet Cinnamon Breadsticks

These sweet-flavored breadsticks can be dipped in cream cheese buttercream. Cream cheese buttercream is a mixture of cream cheese, heavy cream and sweetener.

For the breadstick base:

1 large egg

2 cups mozzarella cheese

¾ cup almond flour

3 tablespoons cream cheese

1 tablespoon psyllium husk powder

1 teaspoon baking powder

For the sweet cinnamon flavorings:

6 tablespoons stevia

3 tablespoons butter

2 tablespoons cinnamon

- Preheat oven to 400 F.
- Mix egg and cream cheese in bowl.
- Mix the dry ingredients: almond flour, psyllium husk powder and baking powder in a separate bowl.
- Microwave mozzarella cheese until sizzling.
- Mix egg, cream cheese and dry ingredients into the mozzarella cheese.
- Mold the dough together and press flat.
- Combine cinnamon sugar flavorings ingredients.
- Put the dough on foil. Cut using a pizza cutter.
- Season with the cinnamon sugar flavorings.
- Bake for 15 minutes. Serve while warm.

PER SERVING: Calories: 292; Fat: 24g; Protein: 13g; Carbs: 7g; Fiber: 4g Net Carbs: 3g; Fat 76% / Protein 19% / Carbs 5%

Ultimate Keto Breadsticks

Serves: 5 / Preparation time: 10 minutes / Cooking time: 20 minutes

You can serve these breadsticks with either marinara sauce or pesto or BBQ sauce or Keto cheese sauce. For the pesto, you can try red pesto, Paleo avocado pesto or basil & macadamia pesto. For the BBQ sauce, you can try spicy chocolate BBQ sauce or blackberry BBQ sauce.

For the breadsticks:

1 cup almond flour

1 cup water (lukewarm)

¾ cup flax meal

¼ cup coconut flour

2 tablespoons psyllium husks (whole)

2 tablespoons chia seeds (ground)

1 teaspoon salt

For the toppings:

2 large egg yolks for brushing

4 tablespoons parmesan cheese (grated)

1 teaspoon sea salt (coarse)

- Mix almond flour, flax meal, coconut flour and psyllium husks in a bowl.
- Add ground chia seeds. Pour water and mix thoroughly.
- Put mixture in the fridge for 20 minutes.
- Preheat oven to 350 F.
- Divide the dough in quarters. Then divide each quarter into 5 pieces.
- Roll and press the dough to form breadsticks.
- Place on a lined baking sheet. Brush with egg yolks.
- Garnish with parmesan cheese and salt.
- Bake for 20 minutes.

PER SERVING: Calories: 334; Fat: 27g; Protein: 13g; Carbs: 16g; Fiber: 12g Net Carbs: 4g; Fat 78% / Protein 17% / Carbs 5%

Low Carb Cheesy Breadsticks

Serve with low sugar marinara sauce. You can be creative with this recipe and add pepperoni or bacon for additional flavor.

For the breadsticks:

4 eggs

1-ounce cream cheese (softened)

1 1/3 cups mozzarella cheese (shredded)

½ cup parmesan cheese (shredded)

1/3 cup coconut flour

4 ½ tablespoons butter (melted and cooled)

1 teaspoon Italian seasoning

½ teaspoon garlic powder

¼ teaspoon baking powder

¼ teaspoon salt

For the toppings:

2 cups mozzarella cheese (shredded)

¼ cup parmesan cheese (shredded)

½ teaspoon Italian seasoning

- Preheat oven to 400 F. Coat baking pan with oil.
- Combine eggs, cream cheese, butter and salt. Mix thoroughly.
- Add coconut flour, baking powder, Italian seasoning and garlic powder. Mix thoroughly.
- Add mozzarella and parmesan cheese to the mixture.
- Pour batter into the coated baking pan.
- Top with mozzarella cheese, parmesan cheese and Italian seasoning.
- Cut into 16 half breadsticks using a pizza cutter.
- Bake for 15 minutes.
- Transfer to the top rack. Broil for 2 minutes.

PER SERVING: Calories: 420; Fat: 31g; Protein: 29g; Carbs: 6g; Fiber: 3g Net Carbs: 3g; Fat 67% / Protein 29% / Carbs 4%

Cheesy Low Carb Garlic Breadsticks

These breadsticks can be served as an appetizer or snacks. It can be served with a white pizza.

For the breadsticks:

2 large eggs

1 ½ cups mozzarella (grated)

1 cup almond flour

¼ cup butter (melted)

3 tablespoons whey protein (unflavored)

2 tablespoons coconut flour

2 teaspoons baking powder

½ teaspoon garlic powder

½ teaspoon salt

For the toppings:

3 tablespoons butter (softened)

2 tablespoons parmesan cheese (grated)

½ teaspoon garlic powder

- Preheat oven to 400 F.
- Mix dry ingredients: almond flour, whey protein, coconut flour, baking powder, garlic powder and salt in a bowl.
- Place mozzarella in a large bowl and melt in a microwave.
- Add eggs, butter and dry mixture into melted mozzarella.
- Place dough ball between 2 large sheets of parchment paper.
- Roll dough to a circle using a rolling pin.
- Remove top sheet of parchment paper.
- Put dough on a baking sheet. Cut into stick size pieces using a pizza cutter.
- Mix all topping ingredients. Spread onto sliced dough.
- Bake for 15 minutes.
- Serve warm.

PER SERVING: Calories: 425; Fat: 34g; Protein: 24g; Carbs: 10g; Fiber: 4g Net Carbs: 6g; Fat 72% / Protein 23% / Carbs 6%

Garlic Breadsticks

Serves: 2 / Preparation time: 10 minutes / Cooking time: 15 minutes

These breadsticks can be dipped with sugar free pasta or pizza sauce. Make sure to create a thick paste when you combine the garlic parmesan butter ingredients.

For the breadsticks:

1 egg

1 ¼ cups mozzarella (shredded)

2 tablespoons coconut flour

1 tablespoon heavy cream

For the garlic parmesan butter:

2 tablespoons butter (melted)

2 tablespoons parmesan cheese

Garlic powder

- Preheat oven to 350 F.
- Melt cheese in a microwave.
- Add egg, coconut flour and heavy cream to the melted cheese.
- Knead dough and roll out between 2 sheets of parchment paper.
- Cut into 6 strips using a pizza cutter. Bake for 15 minutes.
- Mix garlic parmesan butter ingredients.
- Spread onto sliced dough.

PER SERVING: Calories: 369; Fat: 29g; Protein: 19g; Carbs: 7g; Fiber: 4g Net Carbs: 3g; Fat 74% / Protein 23% / Carbs 3%

Cheesy Keto Cauliflower Breadsticks

You can garnish the breadsticks with freshly minced parsley. You can serve the breadsticks with marinara sauce or creamy cheese sauce.

2 large eggs (beaten)

1 ½ cups cauliflower (riced)

1 ½ cups Monterey jack cheese (freshly grated)

½ teaspoon oregano (ground)

½ teaspoon sage (ground)

½ teaspoon thyme (dried)

¼ teaspoon mustard (ground)

Ground black pepper to taste

- Cut cauliflower into florets. Rice using a food processor. Cook for 10 minutes using a microwave oven. Let it cool.
- Preheat oven to 450 F.
- Strain liquid from the riced cauliflower using a kitchen towel. Place in a mixing bowl.
- Add oregano, sage, thyme and mustard. Mix thoroughly.
- Season beaten egg with black pepper. Add to seasoned cauliflower with 3 tablespoons cheese. Mix well.
- Spread cauliflower mixture in a coated baking sheet.
- Use heart-shaped cookie cutter to cut the breadsticks.
- Bake for 10 minutes. Top with ½ cup cheese. Bake for 5 more minutes.
- Let it cool for 3 minutes.

PER SERVING: Calories: 102; Fat: 8g; Protein: 7g; Carbs: 2g; Fiber: 1g
Net Carbs: 1g; Fat 70% / Protein 26% / Carbs 4%

Easy Keto Low Carb Sesame Breadsticks

Serves: 5 / Preparation time: 5 minutes / Cooking time: 20 minutes

Lupin flour is inexpensive compared to organic coconut and almond flours. Lupins are legumes and in the same family as peanuts, if you have a peanut allergy there is a possibility that you also have a lupin allergy. You may use coconut flour as a substitute.

1 medium egg white

¼ cup lupin flour

1 tablespoon olive oil (extra virgin)

1 teaspoon Himalayan pink salt (fine)

½ teaspoon sesame seeds

- Beat the egg white. Add ½ tablespoon olive oil, ½ teaspoon salt and the lupin flour. Mix thoroughly.
- Knead the dough until soft.
- Preheat oven to 320 F.
- Line oven tray with parchment paper. Coat with ½ tablespoon olive oil, ½ teaspoon salt and sesame seeds.
- Divide dough into 5 pieces. Roll and shape into breadsticks.
- Place breadsticks on the oven tray. Roll and coat with oil, salt and sesame seeds.
- Bake for 20 minutes.
- Let it cool and serve.

PER SERVING: Calories: 246; Fat: 17g; Protein: 14g; Carbs: 6g; Fiber: 2g Net Carbs: 4g; Fat 68% / Protein 25% / Carbs 7%

Keto Rosemary and Onion Crackers

Serves: 4 / Preparation time: 10 minutes / Cooking time: 15 minutes

Top these crackers with butter and your favorite cheese. These are moist and crumbly crackers without the grains.

1 large egg

1 cup almonds (ground)

½ cup flax seeds (ground)

2 tablespoons rosemary (chopped)

1 tablespoon olive oil (extra virgin)

1 teaspoon baking soda

½ teaspoon onion powder

1/3 teaspoon black pepper (cracked)

1/3 teaspoon sea salt

- Preheat oven to 340 F.
- Mix dry ingredients: ground almonds, ground flax seeds, chopped rosemary, baking soda, onion powder, salt and pepper in a large bowl.
- Beat the egg with extra virgin olive oil in a separate bowl.
- Add the egg mixture to the dry mixture. Mix thoroughly.
- Roll the dough into a ball. Place between 2 sheets of parchment paper.
- Roll the dough flat using a rolling pin.
- Press out biscuits using a cookie cutter. Place on a baking tray.
- Bake for 15 minutes.
- Let it cool and serve.

**PER SERVING: Calories: 103; Fat: 9g; Protein: 4g; Carbs: 8g; Fiber: 5g
Net Carbs: 3g; Fat 76% / Protein 14% / Carbs 10%**

Keto Cheesy Party Crackers

Serves: 8 / Preparation time: 20 minutes / Cooking time: 40 minutes

Serve these crackers with cheesy bacon dip, salmon pate, guacamole or marinara sauce. These crackers can be stored at room temperature for 5 days or frozen up to 3 months.

1 cup almond flour

1 cup parmesan cheese (grated)

1 cup water

½ cup flax meal

2 tablespoons whole psyllium husks

1 teaspoon salt

¼ teaspoon black pepper

- Mix dry ingredients: almond flour, flax meal, psyllium husks, salt and pepper in a bowl.
- Add grated parmesan cheese. Mix well.
- Pour water and mix well. Let it sit for 15 minutes.
- Preheat oven to 320 F.
- Divide the dough into 2 parts.
- Put half of the dough on parchment paper. Cover with another parchment paper on top. Roll until thin using a rolling pin.
- Fold the dough from the sides to make a rectangular shape. Roll again to flatten.
- Cut dough into 16 pieces using a pizza cutter.
- Repeat the process to the other half of the dough.
- Bake for 40 minutes.

PER SERVING: Calories: 168; Fat: 13g; Protein: 8g; Carbs: 6g; Fiber: 4g Net Carbs: 2g; Fat 75% / Protein 20% / Carbs 5%

Cheesy Grain-free Spinach Crackers

Serves: 16 / Preparation time: 15 minutes / Cooking time: 45 minutes

Serve crackers with salmon pate or guacamole. For crunchier crackers, you may bake for additional 20 minutes at 260 F.

5 ounces spinach (fresh)

1 ½ cups almond flour

½ cup flax meal

½ cup parmesan cheese (grated)

¼ cup butter (softened)

¼ cup coconut flour

½ teaspoon chili peppers (dried and flaked)

½ teaspoon cumin (ground)

½ teaspoon salt

- Boil water in a saucepan over high heat. Add spinach and cook for 1 minute.
- Wash spinach in a bowl of cold water. Strain and squeeze water out of the spinach.
- Place in a food processor. Blend until smooth. Set aside.
- Mix the dry ingredients: almond flour, flax meal, parmesan cheese, coconut flour, chili peppers, cumin and salt in a bowl.
- Add spinach and butter to the dry mixture. Mix thoroughly.
- Wrap dough in a foil. Put in the fridge for 1 hour.
- Preheat oven to 400 F.
- Remove foil and place in a lined baking sheet.
- Cover with another parchment paper on top. Roll until thin.
- Cut the dough into 16 equal pieces using a pizza cutter.
- Bake for 20 minutes.

**PER SERVING: Calories: 126; Fat: 11g; Protein: 5g; Carbs: 4g; Fiber: 3g
Net Carbs: 1g; Fat 80% / Protein 16% / Carbs 4%**

BUNS

Contents

Ultimate Keto Buns

Serves: 10 / Preparation time: 10 minutes / Cooking time: 45 minutes

Top with butter or cream cheese, burger meat or any topping you like. You can mix all dry ingredients ahead of time and store in a zip-lock bag, just add the wet ingredients when ready.

Dry ingredients:

1 ½ cups almond flour

2/3 cup psyllium husks

½ cup coconut flour

½ cup flax meal

5 tablespoons sesame seeds

2 teaspoons cream of tartar

2 teaspoons garlic powder

2 teaspoons onion powder

1 teaspoon baking soda

1 teaspoon salt

Wet ingredients:

6 large egg whites

2 large eggs

2 cups water (boiling)

- Preheat oven to 350 F.
- Mix all dry ingredients in a bowl except for the sesame seeds.
- Add eggs and egg whites. Mix until thick.
- Add boiling water. Mix thoroughly.
- Make buns with a spoon. Put on a baking tray.
- Press sesame seeds on top.
- Bake for 45 minutes.
- Remove from oven. Let it cool.

PER SERVING: Calories: 208; Fat: 15g; Protein: 10g; Carbs: 12g; Fiber: 8g Net Carbs: 4g; Fat 70% / Protein 21% / Carbs 9%

Low Carb Hamburger Buns

Serves: 12 / Preparation time: 10 minutes / Cooking time: 25 minutes

You can use your hands to form the rolls or two muffin top pans to make perfect rounds. Psyllium husk bread can be used with coconut four or almond flour. For a more "classic" presentation, sprinkle the buns with sesame seeds.

2 large eggs

2 cups egg whites

1 cup coconut flour

¾ cup water (warm)

½ cup avocado oil

¼ cup coconut oil

6 tablespoons whole psyllium husks

1 ½ teaspoon baking soda

¾ teaspoon sea salt

- Preheat oven to 350 F. Coat muffin top pan with oil.
- Mix psyllium and water in a small bowl. Set aside.
- Put eggs, egg whites, coconut flour, avocado oil, coconut oil, baking soda and salt in a food processor. Pulse until fully mixed.
- Add psyllium gel and pulse until fully mixed.
- Spoon batter evenly between 12 muffin pans.
- Bake for 30 minutes. Let it sit for 15 minutes.
- Remove from pan and let it cool.

PER SERVING: Calories: 198; Fat: 17g; Protein: 8g; Carbs: 8g; Fiber: 6g Net Carbs: 2g; Fat 78% / Protein 17% / Carbs 5%

Low Carb Bagels

Serves: 6 / Preparation time: 15 minutes / Cooking time: 12 minutes

This is an easy recipe with just 5 ingredients to make. You can add sesame seeds as toppings, just sprinkle and press on the dough before baking.

2 large eggs (beaten)

2 ounces cream cheese (cubed)

2 ½ cups mozzarella cheese (shredded)

1 ½ cups almond flour

1 tablespoon baking powder (gluten-free)

- Preheat oven to 400 F. Line baking sheet with parchment paper.
- Mix almond flour and baking powder. Set aside.
- Combine mozzarella and cream cheese in a bowl. Microwave for 2 minutes.
- Stir halfway through and stir at the end.
- Add flour mixture and eggs to the cheese mixture.
- Use a food processor to mix the dough.
- Place dough on a baking sheet. Divide dough into 6 equal parts.
- Roll and press to make a bagel shape.
- Bake for 10 minutes.

PER SERVING: Calories: 360; Fat: 28g; Protein: 21g; Carbs: 8g; Fiber: 3g Net Carbs: 5g; Fat 71% / Protein 23% / Carbs 6%

Nut-free Keto Buns

Serves: 10 / Preparation time: 15 minutes / Cooking time: 1 hour

Psyllium absorbs water. When baking with psyllium as an ingredient, drink lots of water to avoid constipation.

<u>Dry ingredients:</u>

1 ¼ cups sesame seed flour (fine and defatted)

2/3 cup coconut flour

2/3 cup flax meal

1/3 cup psyllium husk powder

5 tablespoons sesame seeds

2 teaspoons cream of tartar

2 teaspoons garlic powder

2 teaspoons onion powder

1 teaspoon baking soda

1 teaspoon salt

<u>Wet ingredients:</u>

6 large egg whites

2 large eggs

2 ½ cups water (boiling)

- Preheat oven to 350 F.
- Mix all the dry ingredients except for the sesame seeds that will be used for topping in a large bowl.
- Add the egg whites and eggs. Process well using a mixer until thick.
- Add boiling water. Mix thoroughly.
- Form the buns and place on parchment paper.
- Top and press buns with sesame seeds.
- Bake for 1 hour.
- Remove from oven and let it cool for a few minutes.

PER SERVING: Calories: 179; Fat: 11g; Protein: 12g; Carbs: 13g; Fiber: 9g Net Carbs: 4g; Fat 60% / Protein 31% / Carbs 9%

Low Carb Dinner Rolls

Serves: 10 / Preparation time: 5 minutes / Cooking time: 25 minutes

For soft and chewy roll, bake for 20 minutes. For firm and crunchy roll, bake for 35 to 40 minutes.

4 large eggs

¾ cup water

½ cup coconut flour

4 tablespoons butter (melted)

2 tablespoons psyllium husk powder

½ teaspoon baking powder

¼ teaspoon salt

- Combine dry ingredients: coconut flour, psyllium husk powder, baking powder and salt in a bow. Mix well.
- Beat eggs in a separate bowl. Add butter and water. Mix thoroughly.
- Combine dry mixture with the wet mixture. Mix until thick.
- Form 10 dinner rolls and place on a coated baking sheet.
- Bake for 35 minutes at 350 F.

**PER SERVING: Calories: 102; Fat: 7g; Protein: 3g; Carbs: 6g; Fiber: 5g
Net Carbs: 1g; Fat 74% / Protein 20% / Carbs 6%**

Low Carb Gluten and Dairy-free Buns

Serves: 6 / Preparation time: 5 minutes / Cooking time: 26 minutes

These buns can be toasted, frozen and toasted again. You can add butter on top to enjoy as toast.

4 eggs

1 cup almond flour (blanched)

4 tablespoons lard (melted)

1 tablespoon rosemary

1 tablespoon black sesame seeds

1 tablespoon white sesame seeds

1 teaspoon onion flakes

½ teaspoon Himalayan salt

- Preheat oven to 430 F.
- Blend the lard and eggs. Add the rest of the ingredients. Blend well.
- Pour batter into 6 muffin molds. Bake for 26 minutes.
- Let it cool then cut.

PER SERVING: Calories: 230; Fat: 21g; Protein: 8g; Carbs: 4g; Fiber: 2g Net Carbs: 2g; Fat 82% / Protein 14% / Carbs 3%

Keto Burger Buns

Serve with butter and toppings of choice. Bread can be stored in the fridge for later consumption.

3 egg whites

1 ¼ cups almond flour

1 cup water (boiling)

5 tablespoons psyllium husk powder (ground)

2 teaspoons baking powder

2 teaspoons apple cider vinegar

1 teaspoon sea salt

- Preheat oven to 350 F.
- Mix dry ingredients: almond flour, psyllium husk powder, baking powder and salt in a bowl.
- Add egg whites, boiling water, apple cider vinegar. Beat for 30 seconds using a hand mixer.
- Form dough into 6 hamburger buns. Place on a coated baking sheet.
- Bake for 1 hour.

PER SERVING: Calories: 73; Fat: 3g; Protein: 3g; Carbs: 10g; Fiber: 7g
Net Carbs: 3g; Fat 48% / Protein 26% / Carbs 26%

Hamburger Buns

Serves: 5 / Preparation time: 10 minutes / Cooking time: 13 minutes

You can store the burger buns in an airtight container in the fridge for 10 days. Warm buns slightly before consumption.

1 large egg

2 ounces cream cheese

1 ½ cups mozzarella cheese (part skim and grated)

1 ¼ cups almond flour

2 tablespoons oat fiber 500

1 teaspoon baking soda

- Microwave mozzarella cheese and cream cheese for 1 minute. Stir then microwave for 30 seconds more.
- Place the cheese in a food processor and blend with the egg.
- Add the dry ingredients: almond flour, oat fiber and baking soda in the food processor. Blend until dough forms. Place in the freezer for a few minutes.
- Preheat oven to 400 F. Line baking sheet with parchment paper.
- Remove dough from the freezer. Divide into 5 equal pieces.
- Roll each piece into a ball. Put on the parchment paper and flatten.
- Bake for 12 minutes.

PER SERVING: Calories: 294; Fat: 25g; Protein: 14g; Carbs: 7g; Fiber: 3g Net Carbs: 4g; Fat 76% / Protein 19% / Carbs 5%

Sesame Keto Buns

Serves: 12 / Preparation time: 15 minutes / Cooking time: 50 minutes

You can store the buns in the fridge. Toast and top with butter before consumption.

8 egg whites

1 cup coconut flour

1 cup hot water

½ cup psyllium powder

½ cup pumpkin seeds

½ cup sesame seeds + ½ cup to cover the buns

1 tablespoon baking powder (aluminum free)

1 tablespoon sea salt

- Preheat oven to 350 F.
- Combine dry ingredients: coconut flour, psyllium powder, pumpkin seeds, sesame seeds, baking powder and salt in a large bowl. Mix thoroughly.
- Mix egg whites in a blender until very foamy.
- Add the foamy egg whites to the dry mixture. Mix well in a food processor.
- Add 1 cup boiling water to the mixture. Stir until dough becomes smoother.
- Press buns into a plate covered with ½ cup sesame seeds.
- Place buns on a cookie sheet lined with parchment paper.
- Bake for 50 minutes.
- Let it cool in the over for a few minutes before removing.

PER SERVING: Calories: 133; Fat: 7g; Protein: 7g; Carbs: 14g; Fiber: 10g Net Carbs: 4g; Fat 62% / Protein 26% / Carbs 12%

Almond Buns

These almond buns can be used as a breakfast sandwich. It can be an open-faced sandwich or a burger bun.

2 large eggs

5 tablespoons butter (unsalted)

¾ cup almond flour

1 ½ tablespoons baking powder

- Combine dry ingredients: almond flour and baking powder in a bowl. Mix thoroughly.
- Beat the eggs and add in the dry mixture.
- Melt butter and add in the mixture. Mix thoroughly.
- Divide mixture into 6 equal parts. Place in a muffin top pan.
- Bake for 15 minutes at 350 F.
- Let it cool.

PER SERVING: Calories: 373; Fat: 35g; Protein: 10g; Carbs: 7g; Fiber: 3g
Net Carbs: 4g; Fat 85% / Protein 11% / Carbs 4%

Coconut Flour Bread Rolls

Serves: 6 / Preparation time: 45 minutes / Cooking time: 30 minutes

These rolls don't taste like coconut. They taste like other breads, just healthier.

2 whole eggs

2 egg whites

½ cup coconut flour

¼ cup boiling water

4 tablespoons golden flax-seed flour

2 tablespoons coconut oil

2 tablespoons psyllium husk powder

1 tablespoon apple cider vinegar

1 tablespoon baking powder

½ teaspoon salt

- Preheat oven to 350 F. Line baking tray with parchment.
- Combine dry ingredients: coconut flour, flax-seed flour, psyllium husk powder, baking powder and salt in a bowl. Mix thoroughly.
- Add coconut oil and eggs. Blend well until mixture is like breadcrumbs.
- Let it sit for 30 minutes.
- Add apple cider vinegar. Mix thoroughly.
- Add water, a bit at a time and stir.
- Make a ball of dough. Place on the baking tray.
- Bake for 30 minutes.

PER SERVING: Calories: 172; Fat: 10g; Protein: 6g; Carbs: 14g; Fiber: 9g Net Carbs: 5g; Fat 65% / Protein 23% / Carbs 12%

Low Carb Flaxseed and Psyllium Bread Rolls

Serves: 6 / Preparation time: 10 minutes / Cooking time: 30 minutes

These are healthy bread rolls, high in fiber and very filling. You can try it with avocado, tomato and lettuce for lunch.

5 egg whites

2 egg yolks

2 cups golden flaxseed (ground)

½ cup water (boiling)

4 tablespoons olive oil

2 tablespoons apple cider vinegar

2 tablespoons psyllium husk powder

1 tablespoon baking powder

1 teaspoon salt

- Preheat oven to 350 F. Line baking tray with parchment.
- Combine dry ingredients: flaxseed, psyllium husk powder, baking powder and salt in a bowl. Mix thoroughly.
- Add egg whites and egg yolks. Blend well.
- Add oil and apple cider vinegar. Mix thoroughly.
- Add boiling water to the mixture. Mix well. This will result to a slightly sticky mixture.
- Roll dough into 6 balls. Place on the baking tray.
- Bake for 30 minutes.

PER SERVING: Calories: 420; Fat: 34g; Protein: 14g; Carbs: 20g; Fiber: 18g Net Carbs: 2g; Fat 81% / Protein 17% / Carbs 2%

MUFFINS AND CAKES

Contents

Keto 2-Ingredient Muffins

This is an easy recipe that you can use for breakfast. Top with some ghee and enjoy with a cup of coffee.

5 medium eggs (whisked)

2 cups hazelnuts

Stevia and spices to taste

- Preheat oven to 350 F.
- Spray 12-cup muffin tray with oil.
- Put hazelnuts in a food processor. Form a flour.
- Put eggs and hazelnut flour in a large bowl. Mix thoroughly.
- Add stevia and spices to the mixture.
- Pour mixture into the muffin tray.
- Bake for 25 minutes.
- Let it cool before serving.

PER SERVING: Calories: 117; Fat: 10g; Protein: 6g; Carbs: 4g; Fiber: 2g
Net Carbs: 2g; Fat 75% / Protein 19% / Carb 6%

Kale and Chives Egg Muffins

Serves: 4 / Preparation time: 10 minutes / Cooking time: 30 minutes

Enjoy these muffins with a cup of coffee or tea. You can store remaining muffins in the freezer to keep for upcoming breakfasts.

6 eggs

1 cup kale (finely chopped)

½ cup almond milk

¼ cup chives (finely chopped)

Salt and pepper to taste

- Preheat oven to 350 F.
- Beat the eggs. Put kale and chives. Put coconut milk, salt and pepper. Mix thoroughly.
- Spray 8 muffin cups with coconut oil.
- Fill 2/3 of each cup with the mixture.
- Bake for 30 minutes.
- Let it cool for a few minutes then remove from muffin cups.

PER SERVING: Calories: 485; Fat: 42g; Protein: 22g; Carbs: 5g; Fiber: 1g Net Carbs: 4g; Fat 79% / Protein 18% / Carbs 3%

Quick and Easy Keto Egg Muffins

Serves: 12 / Preparation time: 20 minutes / Cooking time: 20 minutes

These egg muffins are high in protein and low in carb can be eaten alone or paired with a smoothie. It can be eaten right after baking and cooling or can be stored and re-heat.

8 ounces pork sausage	½ sweet onion (thinly sliced)
9 eggs	1 tablespoon extra-virgin olive oil
1 ½ cups fresh spinach	1 teaspoon fresh oregano (chopped)
¾ cup red bell pepper (chopped)	¾ teaspoon salt
¼ cup coconut milk	Ground pepper

- Preheat oven to 350 F. Coat muffin tin with oil.
- Heat sausage in a skillet over medium high. Break up sausage with a spatula while cooking.
- Sauté with olive oil, onion, pepper and oregano. Add spinach. Cover and cook for 30 seconds. Remove cover and mix ingredients. Remove from heat.
- Beat eggs, pepper, salt and milk in a large bowl.
- Add the sausage mixture to the egg mixture. Mix thoroughly.
- Pour mixture on 12 coated muffin tins.
- Bake for 20 minutes. Let cool then remove from tins.

**PER SERVING: Calories: 135; Fat: 10g; Protein: 7g; Carbs: 2g; Fiber: 0g
Net Carbs: 2g; Fat 71% / Protein 23% / Carbs 6%**

Paleo Bacon Lemon Thyme Breakfast Muffins

Serves: 12 / Preparation time: 10 minutes / Cooking time: 20 minutes

Lemon thyme can be substituted with other herbs of your choice. This muffin is a great way to start your day with a healthy breakfast.

4 eggs

3 cups almond flour

1 cup bacon bits

½ cup ghee (melted)

2 teaspoons lemon thyme

1 teaspoon baking soda

- Preheat oven to 350 F.
- Place ghee, almond flour, baking soda, eggs and lemon thyme in large bowl. Mix thoroughly.
- Add bacon bits on the mixture.
- Spoon mixture into muffin pan lined with muffin liners.
- Bake for 20 minutes.

PER SERVING: Calories: 300; Fat: 28g; Protein: 11g; Carbs: 7g; Fiber: 3g Net Carbs: 4g; Fat 82% / Protein 13% / Carbs 5%

Keto Lemon Poppy Seed Muffins

Serves: 12 / Preparation time: 10 minutes / Cooking time: 20 minutes

These muffins are easy to make and store in the freezer for a week's breakfast. You can warm them in a microwave for 20 seconds, slice in half and spread with butter.

3 large eggs	¼ cup salted butter (melted)
Zest of 2 lemons	3 tablespoons lemon juice
¾ cup almond flour	2 tablespoons poppy seeds
1/3 cup Erythritol	1 teaspoon baking powder
¼ cup golden flaxseed meal	1 teaspoon vanilla extract
¼ cup heavy cream	25 drops liquid Stevia

- Preheat oven to 350 F.
- Combine almond flour, flaxseed, Erythritol and poppy seeds in a bowl. Mix well.
- Add eggs, heavy cream and butter. Mix until smooth.
- Add baking powder, vanilla, Stevia, lemon zest and lemon juice. Mix thoroughly.
- Spread butter over 12 cupcake molds.
- Bake for 20 minutes.
- Remove from oven. Let it cool for 10 minutes.

**PER SERVING: Calories: 100; Fat: 12g; Protein: 4g; Carbs: 3g; Fiber: 1g
Net Carbs: 2g; Fat 88% / Protein 8% / Carbs 4%**

Chocolate Zucchini Bundt Cake

Serves: 16 / Preparation time: 10 minutes / Cooking time: 1 hour

You can store this cake at room temperature up to 4 days. The moisture coming from the zucchini makes this cake fudgy.

For the cake:

6 large eggs

2 ¾ cups almond flour

1 1/3 cups Erythritol (powdered)

½ cup butter (melted)

½ cup cacao powder

2 teaspoons baking powder (gluten-free)

2 teaspoons vanilla extract (sugar-free)

½ teaspoon sea salt

2 medium zucchini (pureed)

For the frosting:

½ cup cacao powder

¼ cup virgin coconut oil

Stevia drops to taste

- Preheat oven to 325 F. Coat bundt pan with oil.
- Mix dry ingredients: almond flour, Erythritol, cacao powder, baking powder and salt in a bowl.
- Mix wet ingredients: eggs, butter, vanilla extract and zucchini in a separate bowl.
- Pour wet mixture into the dry mixture. Mix thoroughly.
- Pour batter into the coated pan.
- Smooth out top. Bake for 1 hour.
- Let it cool then invert onto a cake stand.
- Melt cacao powder and coconut oil together. Add stevia to taste.
- Pour the frosting over the cake.

PER SERVING: Calories: 228; Fat: 21g; Protein: 7g; Carbs: 8g; Fiber: 4g Net Carbs: 4g; Fat 82% / Protein 11% / Carbs 7%

Pumpkin Bundt Cake

Serves: 12 / Preparation time: 15 minutes / Cooking time: 1 hour

This low carb cake is light and airy coming from the pumpkin puree and eggs. Pumpkin can be swapped with banana or apple for a new recipe.

For the cake:

6 large eggs

2 ¾ cups almond flour

1 1/3 cups Erythritol (powdered)

½ cup butter (melted)

2 teaspoons baking powder (gluten-free)

2 teaspoons pumpkin pie spice

2 teaspoons vanilla extract (sugar-free)

½ teaspoon sea salt

8 ½ ounces pumpkin (puree)

For the glaze:

½ cup Erythritol (powdered)

¼ cup butter (unsalted)

1 teaspoon cinnamon

1 teaspoon vanilla extract (sugar-free)

- Preheat oven to 325 F. Coat bundt pan with oil.
- Mix dry ingredients: almond flour, Erythritol, baking powder, pumpkin pie spice and salt in a bowl.
- Add the wet ingredients: eggs, butter, vanilla extract and pumpkin. Mix until smooth.
- Pour batter into the coated pan.
- Bake for 1 hour.
- Let it cool then put onto a serving platter.
- Combine all glaze ingredients. Cook until melted over low heat.
- Pour the glaze over the cake. Dust with powdered Erythritol.

**PER SERVING: Calories: 289; Fat: 26g; Protein: 8g; Carbs: 8g; Fiber: 3g
Net Carbs: 5g; Fat 82% / Protein 11% / Carbs 7%**

Cinnamon Keto Mug Cake

Serves: 1 / Preparation time: 5 minutes / Cooking time: 5 minutes

You can top with whipped cream or creamed coconut milk and a pinch of cinnamon. To make this recipe nut-free, substitute 2 tablespoons almond flour with 1 tablespoon coconut flour.

1 large egg

2 heaping tablespoons almond flour

1 heaping tablespoon coconut flour

1 tablespoon Erythritol

1 tablespoon extra-virgin coconut oil (melted)

½ teaspoon cinnamon (ground)

1/8 teaspoon baking soda

- Place all dry ingredients: almond flour, coconut flour, Erythritol, cinnamon and baking soda in a mug. Mix well.
- Add the egg and coconut oil. Mix well.
- Microwave on high for 90 seconds.

PER SERVING: Calories: 333; Fat: 29g; Protein: 12g; Carbs: 9g; Fiber: 5g Net Carbs: 4g; Fat 79% / Protein 15% / Carb 6%

Keto Brownie Mug Cake

You can top with whipped cream or creamed coconut milk and or cream fraiche. This is a rich, chocolatey cake that tastes like a brownie.

2 large squares dark chocolate (grated)

1 large egg

¼ cup cacao powder

¼ cup freshly brewed coffee

¼ cup virgin coconut oil (melted)

4 tablespoons Erythritol

2 tablespoons chia seeds (ground)

1 teaspoon baking powder (gluten-free)

½ teaspoon cinnamon

Pinch of sea salt

- Place all the grated chocolate and dry ingredients: cacao powder, Erythritol, chia sees, baking powder, cinnamon and salt in a bowl. Mix well.
- Add the egg, coconut oil and coffee. Mix well.
- Divide mixture between 2 mugs.
- Microwave on high for 90 seconds.

PER SERVING: Calories: 397; Fat: 38g; Protein: 8g; Carbs: 14g; Fiber: 7g Net Carbs: 7g; Fat 85% / Protein 8% / Carb 7%

Keto Eggnog Mug Cake

For added sweetness, you can add 5 drops of liquid Stevia. You can top this with whipped cream or coconut milk and a pinch of cinnamon.

1 large egg

2 heaping tablespoons almond flour

1 heaping tablespoon coconut flour

2 tablespoons Erythritol

1 tablespoon extra-virgin coconut oil (melted)

½ teaspoon rum extract

¼ teaspoon cinnamon (ground)

1/8 teaspoon baking soda

1/8 teaspoon nutmeg (ground)

- Place all dry ingredients: almond flour, coconut flour, Erythritol, cinnamon, baking soda and nutmeg in a mug. Mix well.
- Add the egg, coconut oil and rum extract. Mix well.
- Microwave on high for 90 seconds.

PER SERVING: Calories: 339; Fat: 29g; Protein: 12g; Carbs: 9g; Fiber: 5g Net Carbs: 4g; Fat 79% / Protein 15% / Carb 6%

Measurement Conversion Tables

Volume Equivalents (Liquid)

US Standard	US Standard (ounces)	Metric (Approx.)
2 tablespoons	1 floz	30 ml
¼ cup	2 floz	60 ml
½ cup	4 floz	120 ml
1 cup	8 floz	240 ml
1 ½ cups	12 floz	355 ml
2 cups or 1 pint	16 floz	475 ml
4 cups or 1 quart	32 floz	1 L
1 gallon	128 floz	4 L

Oven Temperatures

Fahrenheit (F)	Celsius (C) (Approx)
250°F	120°C
300°F	150°C
325°F	165°C
350°F	180°C
375°F	190°C
400°F	200°C
425°F	220°C
450°F	230°C

Volume Equivalents (Dry)

US Standard	Metric (Approx.)
¼ teaspoon	1 ml
½ teaspoon	2 ml
1 teaspoon	5 ml
1 tablespoon	15 ml
¼ cup	59 ml
½ cup	118 ml
1 cup	235 ml

Weight Equivalents

US Standard	Metric (Approx.)
½ ounce	15 g
1 ounce	30 g
2 ounces	60 g
4 ounces	115 g
8 ounces	225 g
12 ounces	340 g
16 ounces or 1 pound	455 g

Want MORE full length cookbooks for FREE?

We invite you to sign up for free review copies of future books!

Learn more and get brand new cookbooks for **free:**

http://club.hotbooks.org

Lightning Source UK Ltd.
Milton Keynes UK
UKHW050609070819
347549UK00003B/32/P